# SURVIVING the Storm

## BY AL PITTMAN

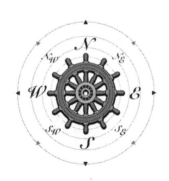

WORD PRODUCTIONS

# SURVIVING
## The Storm

### BY AL PITTMAN

**Published by**
Word Productions LLC
Albuquerque, NM USA
www.wordproductions.org
*Since 1979*


**RESOURCES FROM AL PITTMAN**
**Calvary Worship Center**
505 Castle Road
Colorado Springs, CO 80904-2132
**(719) 632-3311**
www.cwccs.org

# Dedication

*This book is dedicated to the memory of
my father, Al Pittman, Sr.,
who passed away far too soon
on January 19, 1995.
Although not a perfect man, he persevered
through childhood poverty,
racism, war, and life's daily uncertainties.*

*My father modeled for me
an intestinal fortitude,
which has helped to carry me
through many difficulties
in life and ministry.*

*"Thanks dad, I know you did your best."*

# Contents

# Preface

No matter who you are, there will come a time in your life when you are going to face some type of "storm." It might be financial ruin. It might be the loss of someone dear to you. It might be risk to your own life and health. Whatever form it takes, it will shake your faith, splash cold water on your confidence, and upset your vision of how life is going to turn out for you.

It doesn't matter how good or how godly a life you are living. It doesn't matter whether you presently find yourself in a place of relative ease. Storms still have a way of finding you. It's as if they can look you up in the phone book. Storms will find you!

And when a storm *does* find you, expect your life to be changed.

Not long ago, my family and I experienced a devastating storm. It was a beautiful Colorado day, August 4, 2003, and my son Nathan was trying out for the high school football team.

My wife, Norma, and I have three beautiful children: Renee, who at this time was twenty-three years old and married (we're also proud grandparents); Reggie, our youngest, thirteen at the time; and Nathan, who was fourteen years of age when these earth-shattering events took place. This is a day we will never forget.

This was to be Nathan's first year in high school. He loved to play football, and Nathan had dreams, like any fourteen-year-old boy, of playing in the NFL. I happened to have tagged along for his first practice.

Everything was fine. I beamed with pride as I saw my son out on the field going through the various drills, and then it happened. After several sprints up and down the field, Nathan suddenly collapsed. I thought for a moment he was just tired, until I saw one of the coaches frantically waving to another coach as he attended to my son. That's when I sprinted over and found my son struggling for his life.

Nathan's eyes were rolling back into his head, and I had to slap him to keep him awake. He was in excruciating pain and was crying out for water.

In an instant, I went from the mountain peaks of being a proud father into the valley of the shadow of death. We were thrust into the midst of a storm that came on so suddenly and so violently that it shook the very foundation of our faith.

Nathan had contracted something called Rabdomyolosis, a rare illness brought on by severe dehydration, which attacks the muscles.

After six or seven weeks in the hospital Intensive Care Unit, eight major surgeries, and another three weeks of rehabilitation for Nathan's legs, he was able to come home on his birthday, October 1.

Since that time, he is gradually and miraculously recovering from his illness.

My family and I have come to understand something about storms and how to survive them. Like the apostle Paul, I now realize that it's not the size or suddenness of the storm, but the strength and sovereignty of our God who is in the storm with us.

We may think that when trials suddenly come upon us that God has lost control of the situation. But not so! God is always in control. Our plans may change, but God is never surprised. He knows the end from the beginning. And He will help us through every storm that comes upon us.

Life, like the sea, can be unpredictable. Calm can turn into chaos in an instant.

In this book we will be looking at a literal storm that the apostle Paul encountered and survived by relying upon God. During his journey to Rome as a prisoner, a terrible storm descended upon the ship carrying Paul, upsetting the plans of everyone on board. It looked as if they were all destined to find a watery grave at the bottom of the Mediterranean. However, God had other plans.

Could God do a great work in the midst of this horrific storm? Oh yes! And He can do a work in the midst of *your* storm too.

# Part 1

---

## The Calm before the Storm

# Part 1
# The Calm before the Storm

*When it was decided that we should sail to Italy, they delivered Paul and some other prisoners to one named Julius, a centurion of the Augustan Regiment. So, entering a ship of Adramyttium, we put to sea, meaning to sail along the coasts of Asia. Aristarchus, a Macedonian of Thessalonica, was with us. And the next day we landed at Sidon. And Julius treated Paul kindly and gave him liberty to go to his friends and receive care. When we had put to sea from there, we sailed under the shelter of Cyprus, because the winds were contrary. And when we had sailed over the sea which is off Cilicia and Pamphylia, we came to Myra, a city of Lycia. There the centurion found an Alexandrian ship sailing to Italy, and he put us on board.*

*When we had sailed slowly many days, and arrived with difficulty off Cnidus, the wind not permitting us to proceed, we sailed under the shelter of Crete off Salmone.*

*Passing it with difficulty, we came to a place called Fair Havens, near the city of Lasea.*

*Now when much time had been spent, and sailing was now dangerous because the Fast was already over, Paul advised them, saying, "Men, I perceive that this voyage will end with disaster and much loss, not only of the cargo and ship, but also our lives." Nevertheless the centurion was more persuaded by the helmsman and the owner of the ship than by the things spoken by Paul. And because the harbor was not suitable to winter in, the majority advised to set sail from there also, if by any means they could reach Phoenix, a harbor of Crete opening toward the southwest and northwest, and winter there.*

*When the south wind blew softly, supposing that they had obtained their desire, putting out to sea, they sailed close by Crete.*

—Acts 27:1–13

# CHAPTER ONE

# Before the Storm

From time to time, we all face "storms"—trials and difficulties. Big or little, they can change our course in life. They make us wonder what God is doing. They force us to decide whether we will react out of fear or out of faith. We need to learn how to act when such "storms" come upon us.

The apostle Paul encountered a literal storm and came through it with faith that was stronger than ever. His experience with that storm can help us to deal with our own "storms" in life.

For Paul, the story really started a couple of years before the storm, when he was falsely accused of starting a riot at the Jerusalem temple.

Over the months that followed, Paul had pleaded his case before local rulers Felix, Festus, and Agrippa. They refused to release him. Paul, a Roman citizen, had one more card to play: he requested an audience with Caesar (see Acts 21–26).

That's where he was headed when the winds of the storm began to blow.

In the opening verses of Acts 27, what we read about is not the storm itself but the calm *before* the storm.

There are two types of calm before the storm: the worldly "calm" exhibited by the Roman centurion, and the "calm" Paul demonstrated through his faith in God. In order to understand the circumstances Paul found himself in, let's first take a look at the background to this storm.

### The Narrator

Acts 27 reveals much about theology, leadership, ancient shipping practices, and more. But the first thing we should note is who is providing the narration. The very first phrase of the chapter says, "When it was decided that *we* should sail to Italy..."

Who is speaking here? Along with Paul, who is included in the "we"?

According to Scripture, Paul was accompanied on this trip by Aristarchus, a believer from Thessalonica. Earlier, Aristarchus had been arrested in Ephesus, as recorded in Acts 19, and so we know that he had already been through a few trials with Paul. But Aristarchus was not the writer.

Bible scholars tell us that this and the other first-person accounts in Acts point to Luke as the writer of Acts as well as of the Gospel that bears his name. He was a young physician and a partner with Paul. Luke came along with the apostle on this hazardous journey to Rome. The important thing for us to note, then, is that we have an eyewitness account of the storm. We can trust Luke's words fully.

**The Ship and Its People**

Luke gave us some idea of the ship on which Paul set sail as well as the others with him on board.

The centurion named here—Julius—was a member of the Augustan Regiment. The term "Augustan" referred to Caesar Augustus and was an honorary name. The Augustan Regiment was an elite military group. Julius, therefore, must have been an impressive officer.

The prisoners on the ship with Paul were probably a mixture of Romans and non-Romans. Like Paul, there were most likely other Roman citizens on board who were requesting an audience with Caesar. There were probably also non-Roman criminals, condemned by Roman law, who were being transported to Rome to be killed in the arenas as entertainment for the public.

The ship on which the group set sail was from Adramyttium, a seaport on the northwest coast of the Roman province of Asia (modern-day Turkey). As we will see, however, this ship would take the prisoners only part of the way.

## First Stage of the Journey

The storm would not occur until after the ship had already made considerable progress across the Mediterranean Sea. But there were signs of danger early on.

The ship set sail from somewhere on the coast of Israel and headed north, stopping first at Sidon, a port in Phoenicia. By this early date, Paul was already being looked upon favorably by the centurion. "Julius treated Paul kindly and gave him liberty to go to his friends and receive care" (Acts 27:3). Paul may have been in weak health at this time.

From Sidon, the ship sailed north and then west between Cyprus and the southern coast of what is now Turkey. The travelers passed the regions of Cilicia and Pamphylia, stopping at the port of Myra in the region of Lycia. This route protected them from the harsher weather in the center of the Mediterranean.

At Myra, the centurion Julius found a larger ship headed for Italy and transferred Paul and the other prisoners over to it. This ship was one of a fleet of Roman ships that transported grain from Alexandria, Egypt, to Italy. Historians estimate that about 150,000 tons of grain were transported to Italy annually. The ship would have been about 180 feet long, 45 feet wide, and 40 feet deep.

From this point on, the winds were against the travelers. The new ship made slow progress heading westward as far as a point off Cnidus, a city at the southwestern point of Asia (Turkey). The ship then turned south toward Crete. They passed the city of Salmone, located at the eastern end of Crete, then made it as far as a place called Fair Havens, near the center of the southern coast of Crete.

### Paul's Advice

At Fair Havens, Julius apparently convened the men he trusted most and asked their advice about what to do next. Should they stay where they were for the rest of the season, or should they go on?

Because of adverse winds, their progress had been slow. It was already getting well into the fall, when the weather on the Mediterranean Sea could turn treacherous.

Luke pointed out that "the Fast was already over" (Acts 27:9). This was Yom Kippur, the Day of Atonement celebrated by Jews in September or October.

The Mediterranean would not, of course, freeze over in the wintertime. But the waves could become so rough that ships would not be able to cross it.

According to historians, shipping in ancient times was shut down completely from about November 10 to about March 10. It probably wasn't that late in the season for Paul and his companions, but it was already becoming somewhat dangerous for traveling (verse 10):

*Men, I perceive that this voyage will end with disaster and much loss, not only of the cargo and ship, but also our lives.*

At this point, Paul, possibly prompted by the Holy Spirit, felt led to warn his fellow travelers. He had already been traveling. Based on his personal wisdom and knowledge of the sea, he perceived the danger. Later, however, God would reveal to Paul that all on board would survive the journey.

We picture Paul as a great spiritual man—and he was—but he was also a man who never lost touch with reality. In this case, it was as if Paul was saying, "I know I'm on my way to heaven, but I don't want to get there by being dumb." He used his common sense, based on his considerable experience as a traveler. Paul wanted to stay put, but the others wanted to press on.

## Julius's Decision

As it turned out, Paul's view was in the minority. The majority, including the helmsman and the owner of the ship, wanted to sail on at least as far as Phoenix, a better harbor located at the western end of Crete. There they could spend the winter more comfortably.

The helmsman took Julius's nautical advice over Paul's, confidently believing he could steer the ship as far as Phoenix.

The ship's owner may have sweetened the pot financially. He may have said something like "Here is a little something extra for you, Julius, if you will take us to Phoenix."

Maybe Julius himself had reasons for going on. Maybe he was tired and wanted to get home as soon as possible. He may have had a family waiting for him. In any case, Julius decided not to take Paul's advice. It was a decision they would all come to regret.

**Trusting the Truth**
The decision-making process here is like a commentary of the carnal mind of man. Paul was telling the truth about the dangers they faced, but Julius ignored it. In the same way, people today don't always want to hear the truth; they want to hear what they want to hear.

The Bible says, "Faithful are the wounds of a friend" (Proverbs 27:6). In other words, friends will tell you the truth you need to know, because they care about you. Even if it hurts to hear it, the truth proves to be good for you in the end.

Paul based his advice on the signs of worsening weather. The centurion saw the signs but chose to go on anyway.

At first it looked like the centurion had made a good choice. "When the south wind blew softly, supposing that they had obtained *their desire,* putting out to sea, they sailed close by Crete" (Acts 27:13). But their desire was not God's desire.

The calm was about to come to an end.

# Worldly Calm

The people on board the ship experienced a period of calm just before the
storm hit. In this chapter, we will study
this first type of calm before the "storm."
The centurion experienced something I call
the "false calm." He trusted in his
*assumptions* based on circumstances,
and his assumptions led to a false peace.

### Missed Signs

The centurion rejected the counsel of Paul
and embraced the counsel of the expert
(helmsman) and the owner of the ship. In
doing so, he ignored the signs that would
have confirmed the fact that Paul was
right. Julius ignored these four signs:

1. "The winds were contrary" (Acts 27:4).

2. They "arrived with difficulty off Cnidus" (verse 7).

3. They passed Salmone "with difficulty" (verse 8).

4. "Sailing was now dangerous" (verse 9).

This should have made them at least cautious, and yet they sailed on. Why? The centurion chose to sail on because he placed his trust in circumstances rather than God. The south wind was blowing; maybe the sun was on his face; and with no storm in sight, he must have thought, *You know, I think we can make it.*

But circumstances were going to change suddenly.

## Deceptive Calm

It's amazing how deceptive outward calm can be. For example, sometimes people think that since God has not brought judgment on their life, He must be sleeping or must have forgotten all about their sins. But God's calm is really an act of mercy toward us.

Do you have money in the bank and relative ease in life? Do you look around yourself and think, *Hey, everything's going great?* Jesus spoke of a rich man who felt this way (Luke 12:20). Jesus referred to him as a "fool." Because of this man's boasting, his life would be required of him.

The church at Laodicea thought they were in great shape too. And by worldly standards, they were. But their material wealth said nothing about their spiritual condition.

Here are the strong words of Jesus for the Laodicean church:

*Because you say, "I am rich, have become wealthy, and have need of nothing"—and do not know that you are wretched, miserable, poor, blind, and naked—I counsel you to buy from Me gold refined in the fire, that you may be rich; and white garments, that you may be clothed, that the shame of your nakedness may not be revealed; and anoint your eyes with eye salve, that you may see.* Revelation 3:17–18

God was looking at their hearts, not their bank accounts.

Outward calm in our circumstances is not the rule by which we measure our relationship with God.

Many people are like the Roman centurion when it comes to their relationship with God: they ignore the signs. They ignore the works of Jesus, the miracles He performed, and the prophecies He fulfilled. They ignore the sign of the cross. They ignore the empty tomb. They ignore it all—but that will never change the course of God's just judgment from bearing down upon this earth.

Hebrews 4:13 says, "There is no creature hidden from His sight, but all things are naked and open to the eyes of Him to whom we must give account." We have to deal with God. He will not be ignored. Choosing to ignore the warning signs from God can prove to be disastrous. Pay attention to the signs. Pay attention to the Holy Spirit. He was sent into the world to warn us—to convict us of sin, of righteousness, and of judgment (John 16:7-11).

## Our Desire, God's Desire

When the south wind began to blow, the centurion, the helmsman, and the owner assumed they would obtain their desire. But they were wrong.

Similarly, it is false for us to think that receiving what we want in life means that God is blessing us.

God wants us to be blessed and to enjoy good things in life. After all, "the earth is the Lord's, and all its fullness" (Psalm 24:1). There's nothing wrong with prosperity per se. But comparing worldly prosperity with godly prosperity is nothing more than a false assumption.

In the past I've spoken to some so-called believers who have abandoned their marriage covenants and have arrogantly claimed, "I'm closer to the Lord now than I've ever been." What they mean is that they "feel good" because their outward circumstances have changed. They have attained "their desires." They suppose that because they "feel happy" God must approve of what they have done. That's not true.

I don't mean to pick on people who are divorced, and I realize that sometimes there are biblical reasons for divorce. But this point should be made: sometimes we disobey God and then, to justify our behavior, we point to our worldly prosperity and declare, "All is well." That's always a mistake.

The centurion and the helmsman supposed that they had obtained their desire by sailing toward Phoenix (Acts 27:13). Jesus told a story about a man who lived his life solely based on his circumstances:

> *The ground of a certain rich man yielded plentifully. And he thought within himself, saying, "What shall I do, since I have no room to store my crops?" So he said, "I will do this: I will pull down my barns and build greater, and there I will store all my crops and my goods. And I will say to my soul, 'Soul, you have many goods laid up for many years; take your ease; eat, drink, and be merry.'" But God said to him, "Fool! This night your soul will be required of*

*you; then whose will those things be which you have provided?" So is he who lays up treasure for himself, and is not rich toward God.* (Luke 12:16-21)

We may attain our desires and lay up treasure for ourselves, but if we have ignored God, we are nothing more than fools.

Is a south wind blowing for you? You might be driving the car you want to drive and living where you want to live and making the money you like to make. But is it well with your soul? Jesus said in another place, "What profit is it to a man if he gains the whole world, and is himself destroyed or lost?" (Luke 9:25).

Just like the rich man in Jesus's story, the helmsman, the ship's owner, and the centurion thought they had obtained their desire. But obtaining our desire is worthless in comparison to obtaining the desire of God. Only when we obtain the desire of God, which is a relationship with God through Christ, are we truly rich.

Jesus said, "He who finds his life will lose it, and he who loses his life for My sake will find it" (Matthew 10:39). Yet many people are trying to hold on to their life and are trying to obtain their desire, desires that cannot sustain them in a storm.

## Delighting in God

Psalm 37:4 is a popular verse for Christians to quote.

> Delight yourself also in the Lord,
>   And He shall give you the desires
>     of your heart.

But note that the operative word here is "delight." We receive the desires of our heart only when we first delight ourselves in God.

If God took everything of worldly value away from you today, could you still have delight?

God will grant us the desire of our heart if He is the primary desire of our heart.

This brings us to the second calm represented in Paul's journey towards the storm. While the centurion focused on worldly circumstances, Paul placed his trust in God.

22

# CHAPTER THREE

# The Calm of Faith

What amazes me about Paul in this story is his humility. He knew what was coming, and he did his best to warn the leader, but when he was overruled, he remained quiet.

Paul had failed to persuade Agrippa and the other rulers back in Israel about his innocence. He failed to persuade the centurion not to sail any farther. At this point he could have said, "Ah, I quit." But he didn't. He remained calm, continually trusting in God. This is the calm of faith.

When I see "storms" (trials) coming in my life, my inclination is to try to escape them. I begin to think, "Lord, take me over that situation or around it, because I don't want to go through it." I don't want to confront difficult people. I don't want to deal with troublesome situations.

We would all love for our lives to be peaceful all the time. In fact, the Bible exhorts, "As much as depends on you, live peaceably with all men" (Romans 12:18). But sometimes "as much as depends on you" is not enough.

Sometimes there's a "storm"—a confrontation or something—coming, and as much as we'd like to go over it or around it, God takes us through it.

That's when we need true calmness— calmness based on faith in a faithful God.

## A Life on the Rock

Paul knew the storm was coming. Probably Aristarchus and Luke (Paul's companions) knew it as well. But Paul stayed on the ship. He didn't jump overboard, trying to swim with his chains on. He didn't stir up the other men to mutiny. He stayed on the ship. Why? Because Paul was confident that God is faithful even when people are foolish.

Be calm and know that God is faithful and God is in charge.

*Let my faith be Rock Solid.*

Paul's life had a solid foundation. As Jesus said,

> *Whoever hears these sayings of Mine, and does them, I will liken him to a wise man who built his house on the rock: and the rain descended, the floods came, and the winds blew and beat on that house; and it did not fall, for it was founded on the rock. But everyone who hears these sayings of Mine, and does not do them, will be like a foolish man who built his house on the sand: and the rain descended, the floods came, and the winds blew and beat on that house; and it fell. And great was its fall.* Matthew 7:24-27

Paul's house was built on the rock. And it didn't matter what flood might come or what wind might blow against his house. His house—his life—would stand because he was firmly fitted on the rock of Jesus Christ.

## Hearing and Doing

The key for us is in Jesus's words "Whoever hears these sayings of Mine, *and does them…*" (Matthew 7:24). A lot of Christians hear the Word of God week after week, and some of us even teach the Word, but we may neglect to *do* God's Word. If we just hear it and don't do it, we will discover that faith without works produces death (James 2:26).

Many years ago, a well-known television evangelist fell into sin. Although he was a teacher of the Word, he was not a doer. He's back on television now, but something has changed.

If we are not willing to do what God's Word says, the storm of temptations and trials will wash our faith right out the door.

Many Christians think faith is useless. They say, "This stuff doesn't work." But when you ask them, "Are you praying? Are you standing on God's Word? Are you being diligent to do the things that God has shown you to do?" They will more than likely have to answer, "No."

If we're honest, often we are looking for some magic formula to drop out of heaven and make us a super Christian, curing all our problems and delivering us from every storm.

We live in a day when there is a copious amount of Bible teaching on television, radio, and seminars available within the Church. Yet we are not acting on what we have heard.

God will leave us in a state of stagnation until we obey Him, and only then will He move us on.

Paul was standing on the rock of God's Word. He knew the storm was coming, but he was not concerned with the severity of the storm. He was more concerned with his position in Christ. He wanted to be found standing on the rock, resting in God's love.

**The Cushion of Faith**

I once read a story about a submarine that was being tested. It had been submerged for several hours. When it returned to harbor, the captain was asked, "How did the terrible storm last night affect you?"

The officer looked at his questioner in surprise and said, "Storm? We didn't even know there was a storm."

The sub had been so far beneath the surface that it had reached an area known to sailors as "the cushion of the sea." At that depth, although the ocean may be whipped into huge waves by great winds, the waters below are never stirred.

A. T. Pierson said, "The peace of God is that eternal calm which lies far too deep in the praying, trusting soul to be reached by any external disturbance."

People who live on the surface all their lives and are tossed to and fro by the waves of the sea will never understand the peace of God. The roots of their faith have never gone deep. They are sort of into Christianity because to them it is a fad and a way to get "stuff" from God. They have never truly allowed the Holy Spirit to get"stuff" out of them. They never come to comprehend what I call "the cushion of faith."

**Abide in the Secret Place**
There's a cushion for each one of us within the depth of our soul. The Bible says that if we seek God diligently, we will find Him (Jeremiah 29:13). We will discover His secret place.

Psalm 27:5 says,

*In the time of trouble*
    *He shall hide me in His pavilion;*
*In the secret place of His tabernacle*
    *He shall hide me;*
*He shall set me high upon a rock.*

What is that "secret place"? According to Psalm 31:20, it is God's presence. Our desire must be to know Him. How do we come into His presence? The Bible says we enter His gates with thanksgiving and His courts with praise (Ps.100:4). We access the presence of God by obeying the Word of God—by doing the things that we have heard in God's Word.

In Leviticus 9, Moses declared to His people that if they would obey His Word He would manifest His presence. Where there is a lack of spiritual depth there will always be a of a lack of obedience. We must obey in order to stay in the cushion of faith.

## A Matter of Focus

Paul was a doer. Paul trusted in God, and so the presence of God was with him. I believe that during the storm in Acts 27, the Lord was ministering to Paul, yet Paul had no idea at the outset how severe the storm was going to be. He did not find out until about three days into the storm, when an angel of the Lord assured him that he would survive (Acts 27:23).

When we encounter "storms" in life, we often focus on the "storm" rather than on God. We are then dealing with the situation in our own strength from a position of fear. But God is saying to us, "Don't focus on the sea and the waves. Focus on Me." In other words, He is the Creator of the sea and reigns supreme over the storm. The psalmist declares,

*Who is mighty like You, O Lord?...*
*You rule the raging of the sea;*
*When its waves rise, You still them.*
Psalm 89:8-9

You don't have to fear the storm when you know the God who rules over the storm. Paul did not focus on his position, circumstances, or weaknesses, but on Christ's position as Ruler over the sea.

The God of the Old Testament is the God of the New Testament. Jesus stood up in a boat after being awakened by His disciples and rebuked them for their lack of faith, then commanded the waves and the wind to cease (Matthew 8:23-27). You don't have to worry about the storm when you know the One who is able to still the storm. We must recognize, by faith, God's sovereignty over the storm.

## Faith Is the Issue

Sometimes, on the other side of a storm, I can look back and say, "Oh, I see what the Lord was doing." But when I'm going through a storm, I don't have a clue what God is doing. But at that time, it's not essential that I know "why" but rather "who." Faith seeks the who of the storm.

"Lord, how severe is the storm going to get?" we ask. "When is the storm going be over, Lord?" That's not the issue. The issue is one of faith, one of trusting in Him. Our job is to know the One who has dominion over the storm, not to know the storm.

Newly elected president Abraham Lincoln faced disunion and war. Nobody knew how things were going to turn out for the nation. On February 11, 1861, as he was leaving his hometown of Springfield, Illinois, to take office, he was quoted as saying:

> "My friends—No one, not in my situation, can appreciate my feeling of sadness at this parting. To this place, and the kindness of these people, I owe everything. Here I have lived a quarter of a century, and have passed from a young to an old man. Here my children have been born, and one is buried. I now leave, not knowing when, or whether ever, I may return, with a task before me greater than that which rested upon Washington. Without the assistance of that Divine Being, who ever attended him, I cannot succeed. With that

assistance I cannot fail. Trusting in Him, who can go with me, and remain with you and be every where for good, let us confidently hope that all will yet be well. To His care commending you, as I hope in your prayers you will commend me, I bid you an affectionate farewell."

Abraham Lincoln trusted in the same God Paul trusted. Though he was in the calm before the storm, he was willing to face his adversary and the challenge of a divided nation with the help of God.

The prophet Isaiah declared to God:

*You will keep him in perfect peace,*
    *Whose mind is stayed on You,*
        *Because he trusts in You.*
            Isaiah 26:3

If we keep our minds on Him, no matter what is swirling around us, God is able to keep us in perfect peace. The challenge is to keep focused on Him, maintaining a focus based on faith and not feelings.

In the next chapter, I am going to give you three steps that will help you keep your mind focused on God through the storm. I believe these steps will enable you to experience God's calm as you live in the confusion of today's world. They will help you experience God's presence on a daily basis whether there is a storm or not.

# CHAPTER FOUR

# Three Steps to Calmness

In our fast-paced society, in order to experience the peace of God we must take time for God. You may say, "What!? There are things I've got to do. I can't slow down." Yes, you can. And I'll tell you how: through prayer. Trying to experience the peace of God without time with God is like trying to stop a car traveling one hundred miles per hour without brakes. Calmness in a storm comes to us as a result of our spiritual walk before and during the storm.

## Step 1: Slow Down

Prayer has a way of setting our priorities straight. The fluff—whatever isn't really important—goes by the wayside. We start focusing more on people and relationships and things that are essential to our relationship with the Lord.

Furthermore, when we pray, it counters the inward storm of anxiety we must contend with. As Paul said to the Philippians,

*Be anxious for nothing, but in everything by prayer and supplication, with thanksgiving, let your requests be made known to God; and the peace of God, which surpasses all understanding, will guard your hearts and minds through Christ Jesus* Philippians 4:6-7

An anonymous author has penned this prayer, which is pertinent to the needs of many Christians today.

*Slow me down, Lord. Ease the pounding of my heart by quieting my mind. Steady my harried, hurried pace. Give me calmness amid the confusion of my day. Break the tension of my nerves with soothing music of thy love that lives in my memory. Teach me the art of taking minute vacations to pray for a friend or to look at some beauty of nature. Help me to realize there is more to my Christian life than speed. Let me look upward toward the branches of the towering oak and remember that it grew great and strong because it grew slowly. Slow me down, Lord, slow me down.*

Prayer must be a priority. It's not our theology that will get us through the storm, but "knee-ology." "Seek first the kingdom of God and His righteousness, and all these things shall be added to you" (Matthew 6:33).

### Step 2: Cease to Be Reactionary

When I'm in a crisis, the first thing I want to do is react—I want to get busy and do something.

One way we can experience God's calm in the midst of a storm is to refuse to react immediately to a crisis. The great F. B. Meyer gave some sound advice along these lines:

> Never act in panic, nor allow man to dictate to you. Calm yourself and be still. Force yourself into the quiet of your closet until the pulse beats normally and the scare has ceased to

disturb. When you are most eager to watch or to act is the time when you make the most pitiable mistakes.

Do not ask or do not say in your heart what you will or will not do but wait upon God until he makes known his way. So long as that way is hidden, it is clear that there is no need of action, that he accounts himself responsible for all results of keeping you where you are.

We find the same advice in Scripture. In Ecclesiastes 5:2-3, Solomon writes:

*Do not be rash with your mouth,*

*And let not your heart utter anything hastily before God.*

*For God is in heaven, and you on earth;*

*Therefore let your words be few.*

*For a dream comes through much activity,*

*And a fool's voice is known by his many words.*

In other words, "Be quiet and listen." Don't always have your mouth running about something, certainly about things you don't even understand. Be quiet. Be still and know that He is God and we are not! Don't be reactionary, but rather be a revolutionary, revolting against the dictates of the flesh and yielded in obedience to the Spirit of God.

## Step 3: Experience the Peace of God

We can experience the calm of God in the approaching storm when we enthrone the Son of God within our hearts.

For some people, the "storm" will always be bigger than God because their God is small. But if God is the One who created the heavens and the earth, and if He holds the universe in His hands (Isaiah 40:12), then we can trust Him to preserve that which we have committed to Him... even through a storm.

God has performed great miracles on our behalf. He has given us salvation. We ought to be jumping up and down just because of that! But then God has also placed His glory inside us. As we look back on our lives, we can remember the many things God has done for us in specific situations.

But then we run into a new problem and once again we find ourselves wondering, *Can God deliver me out of this?*

Although God has spiritually "parted the Red Sea for us," we often find ourselves drowning in a ditch. We know God can do anything, yet we find ourselves doubting His willingness. Unbelief robs us of God's peace.

We become convinced we're drowning when in fact it's only a ditch. We cry out, "Lord, why won't you help? I'm drowning!" That's when God simply whispers, "Stand up."

I think God has a sense of humor. I can imagine the Lord answering us immediately, saying, "Yeah, isn't it amazing? When you stand on My Word, you don't have to live in the mud of doubt and unbelief."

What appears to be an ocean of trouble to us is merely a shallow mud puddle to God. So don't wallow in it!

Romans 8:32 says, "He who did not spare His own Son, but delivered Him up for us all, how shall He not with Him also freely give us all things?" As believers we have free access to the holy presence of God. His presence is not diminished by the storms in our lives. If we will draw near to Him in the storm, He will draw near to us (James 4:8). We can experience His presence in the storm if we will reflect upon His past faithfulness, choosing to stand on the promises of His Word rather than in the muck and mire of unbelief.

In the next section of this book we're going to look at "Surviving the Storm." But first, do a little self-evaluation. Where are you today? Maybe you're facing an impending "storm" and you're worried about how severe it's going to be. Know that God is with you in that "storm," that He reigns over the "storm." We can experience His presence, His peace, and His love if we will search for Him in earnest, with all of our hearts (Deuteronomy 4:29).

**The Five Principles for Survival**

In Acts 27 we find five principles for survival that we can implement in our lives when we go through a storm. In the next five chapters of this book we will study those principles. The first of these five principles is to jettison excess weight. In the next chapter, I will teach you what that means.

These five principles are going to help you remain close to God through your storms and help you to ride on the life preserver of God's Word through every storm to survival.

# Part 2

## Survival in the Storm

# Part 2
## Survival in the Storm

*Not long after, a tempestuous head wind arose, called Euroclydon. So when the ship was caught, and could not head into the wind, we let her drive. And running under the shelter of an island called Clauda, we secured the skiff with difficulty. When they had taken it on board, they used cables to undergird the ship; and fearing lest they should run aground on the Syrtis Sands, they struck sail and so were driven. And because we were exceedingly tempest-tossed, the next day they lightened the ship. On the third day we threw the ship's tackle overboard with our own hands. Now when neither sun nor stars appeared for many days, and no small tempest beat on us, all hope that we would be saved was finally given up.*

*But after long abstinence from food, then Paul stood in the midst of them and said, "Men you should have listened to me, and not have sailed from Crete and incurred this disaster and loss. And now I urge you to take heart, for there will be no loss of life among*

*you, but only of the ship. For there stood by*
*me this night an angel of the God to whom*
*I belong and whom I serve, saying, 'Do not*
*be afraid, Paul; you must be brought before*
*Caesar; and indeed God has granted you all*
*those who sail with you.' Therefore take*
*heart, men, for I believe God that it will be*
*just as it was told me. However, we must*
*run aground on a certain island."*

—Acts 27:14-26

# CHAPTER FIVE

# Survival Principle 1:

## JETTISON EXCESS WEIGHT

In one of the old Sylvester Stallone *Rocky* movies, the character Rocky is facing a fierce opponent. This challenger for the heavyweight boxing championship of the world has an intimidating appearance with muscles bulging out everywhere. He stares Rocky (the reigning champion) down.

Before the start of the match, the emcee announces Rocky's measurements, his weight and height, as well as those of his opponent. It is apparent that Rocky is a lot smaller than his challenger. The drama builds and the two boxers meet in the center of the ring.

Rocky's opponent looks into Rocky Balboa's eyes and says, "I'm going to bust you up."

What does Rocky do? He gets right up in his opponent's face, looks him straight in the eye, and says, "Go for it." He is not about to back down. That's what we need to do in the storms of life.

Consider the apostle Paul, who, when up against overwhelming odds, stood up to the challenges he faced in this very intimidating storm.

Are you in the midst of a "storm"? Feeling overwhelmed? Don't give up! With God in your corner, you're already victorious. However, like any successful boxer, what we need is a survival strategy.

### The Storm Arrives

In part one of this book, we looked at the calm before the storm of Acts 27. The centurion Julius decided to take advantage of a favorable south wind to try to make it to a better harbor at Crete's western end.

The Bible says, "Not long after, a tempestuous head wind arose, called Euroclydon" (Acts 27:14). Euroclydon was a sailor's term for a wind blowing from northeast. This wind blew the ship away from the island of Crete and out into the middle of the sea.

There wasn't much the ship's crew could do at this point. They could not head back toward Crete against the wind, so they just let the storm blow them where it would. The wind was overwhelming.

At one point they passed under the ledge of a small island named Clauda, fifty miles off the southern coast of Crete. This gave the crew a chance to make preparations for riding out the storm. First, they pulled the skiff (lifeboat)—which normally trailed the ship on a cable—onto the ship's deck and secured it there for a time when they might want to use it. Second, they tied ropes around the ship to help it hold together better. Third, they took down their sails, since they were afraid of running aground on the Syrtis Sands, a large sandbar that extends from northern Africa.

The next day, with some relief from the storm, they took further measures. They began lightening the ship by throwing nonessential items overboard.

They grew so desperate the following day that they even threw overboard the ship's tackle. This was the rigging for the ship, that which raised and lowered the sails. They took this measure even though it meant they had less ability to guide the ship.

Even after doing all this, the ship remained at the mercy of the storm. Luke reported, "Now when neither sun nor stars appeared for many days, and no small tempest beat on us, all hope that we would be saved was finally given up" (verse 20). Paul was on a ship of "no hope."

**Get Rid of It!**
The crew of the ship Paul was traveling on threw overboard everything they could in a desperate attempt to keep the ship afloat. Cargo, rigging, personal belongs—it didn't matter. The issue was weight, and it was essential that they get rid of it in order to survive the raging storm.

Many times God will allow a crisis into peoples' lives to rid them of the weight that hinders their relationship with Him. God will bring us all to a place where we must jettison (cast off) those things that hold us back from knowing Him or drawing closer to Him. The writer of Hebrews declared: "Let us lay aside every weight, and the sin which so easily ensnares us, and let us run with endurance the race that is set before us, looking unto Jesus, the author and finisher of our faith" (Hebrews 12:1-2). God doesn't want us to get rid of some of the weight; He wants us to lay aside "every weight," most definitely including "the sin which so easily ensnares us."

Storms have a way of bringing us back to the basics. And getting back to basics is what we must do to survive the storm.

**Joseph Cast Off His Coat**

One Bible character who was willing to jettison or cast off, this excess weight was Joseph. We read the story in Genesis 39. Joseph had been sold into slavery by his brothers, was taken down to Egypt, and ended up in the household of an Egyptian official named Potiphar.

One day Joseph and Potiphar's wife were alone in the house together, and she grabbed him by his coat and said, "Lie with me." Now, that's temptation! But Joseph resisted. He ran away, leaving behind his coat in order to escape Potiphar's wife's lustful grip.

Potiphar's wife would go on to accuse Joseph of trying to rape her.

The point is, Joseph didn't hesitate to leave his coat behind. He was willing to get rid of whatever might hinder him from obeying God.

Can you imagine Joseph negotiating with God about the coat? When Potiphar's wife grabbed him, he could have said to God, "I ought to get out of here, but this is a nice coat, Lord. I mean, that coat was the last one on the rack. It cost a lot of money!" Rationalizing can cause our demise and our defeat in a storm.

It sounds foolish. Joseph didn't negotiate about his coat. It didn't matter what the coat cost. The only thing that mattered to him was that he obey God. Joseph was willing to leave behind his coat but not his integrity.

Satan wants us to do the opposite. He wants us to hang on to those things that keep us bound. Many people have left their integrity behind...for the "coat."

Think about the words of Joseph, who said to his master's wife, "Look, my master does not know what is with me in the house [he trusts me], and he has committed all that he has to my hand. There is no one greater in this house than I, nor has he kept back anything from me but you, because you are his wife. How then can I do this great wickedness, and sin against God?" (Genesis 39:8-9).

Joseph was more concerned about his relationship with God than about enjoying sin for a season. In other words, Joseph was saying by his actions, "It is impossible for me to hold on to this 'weight' and please God at the same time. And if this coat is holding me back from pleasing my Father, then you can have it!" He slipped out of his coat and left it there.

**Negotiating with God**

Joseph didn't try to negotiate with God about keeping the coat. But we often try. Why, in the midst of a storm, do we tend to negotiate over the weights that drag us down?

God knows what needs to go and what needs to stay. Thus, if we find ourselves negotiating with God in a storm, it may be a clear indication that we are caught up in idolatry, exposing a life of compromise. Let us not grieve the Holy Spirit but rather give the Spirit sovereignty over the inventory of our hearts.

## A Trial Longer than Necessary

John Bevere, in his video sermon entitled "The Bait of Satan," made this statement: "You cannot shorten your time of testing, but you can extend it." When we refuse to let go of those things that compromise our faith we can actually prolong the duration of the storm.

We must be willing to throw overboard every weight and those things that so easily ensnare us. I have my list of those things; what's yours? Have you given that list to the Holy Spirit?

## Jettison the Weight, Now!

Are you willing to surrender all, jettisoning everything from your life that hinders your relationship with God? If you're in such a place, then rejoice! It's time to throw it overboard in Jesus' name. Simply confess: "Lord, here is the excess weight. I give it to You. I refuse to carry it any longer."

**Good News**

God often brings us to a point of desperation, as He did the sailors in Acts 27. Can you imagine being on a ship smaller than a cruise ship, which has been tossed about on the sea all night and all day, for three days? What would it have been like to have seen neither sun nor stars for three days? Luke writes, "All hope that we would be saved was finally given up" (Acts 27:20).

Have you given up hope? Are you in despair, at the end of your rope? Have you reached the point of saying, "I can't take another step"?

I've got good news for you. You are exactly where God wants you to be! God brings us to the point of desperation because He knows that only desperate people can be delivered.

Many Christians go to church every week but have lost their sense of desperation for Jesus. Oh, they like the sermon and the music's pretty good, and they may even feel better as a result of going, but as soon as the last chorus is sung, they return to living a life lacking any sincere desire to know Jesus.

The Lord God declared to the prophet Ezekiel, "Indeed you are to them as a very lovely song of one who has a pleasant voice and can play well on an instrument; for they hear your words, but they do not do them" (Ezekiel 33:32).

Desperate people will hang on to the Word of God as if it's a life preserver. They've got to have God. Nothing but God will satisfy them. They've come to a place in their life where Jesus is everything to them. They've gone beyond the point of hearing only.

Someone said, "You won't know Jesus is everything until you've lost everything." God brings us to a place of desperation, that He might bring about restoration.

Let us rid ourselves of every weight and cleave to Jesus alone, holding fast to Him through prayer and the promises of His Word (Psalm 4:8). "I will both lie down in peace, and sleep; for You alone, O LORD, make me dwell in safety" (Psalm 4:8).

# CHAPTER SIX

# Survival Principle 2:

## REMEMBER THAT GOD IS WITH YOU

Knowing that God is with you in the "storm" will keep your head above water. "You, O Lord, are...the One who lifts up my head" (Psalm 3:2).

### The Presence of God

We learn about this second principle in something Paul said to the others on board the ship. Paul said he had received a very special visitor: "an angel of the God to whom I belong and whom I serve" (Acts 27:23).

This kind of visitation was not unprecedented. A similar phrase is used to describe the visitor who confronted Joshua (Judges 2:1). And this is the same being described as "the Angel of His Presence" in Isaiah 63:9. The idea of having God stand by His people also appears in 2 Timothy 4:17, where Paul described how the Lord had strengthened him when he was opposed by Alexander the coppersmith.

The same Lord stood by Paul when he was in the storm, tossed about in this vessel of hopelessness. In our darkest hour we can be assured that God is there.

## Father on Deck

Years ago, the captain of a large vessel set sail with his family from Liverpool, their destination being New York. One night, when everyone was asleep, a storm arose. The wind came sweeping over the decks, and the vessel almost capsized. Many people sprang from their beds and didn't know what to do.

The captain's daughter, just eight years old, was awakened and cried with fright. She asked, "What's the matter?" And when they had told her about the storm, she asked one more question: "Is Father on deck?"

They assured her that her father was on deck, and so she dropped back onto her pillow without any fear showing on her face. Despite the howling winds and crashing waves, she was soon fast asleep. Why? Because she knew her *Father* was on deck.

Is God with you in your "storm"? Yes, He is. Your Father is on deck. God is in charge of the situation. His presence brings a calm assurance (2 Chronicles 20:9). "If disaster comes upon us—sword, judgment, pestilence, or famine—we will stand before this temple and in Your presence (for Your Name is in this temple), and cry out to You in our affliction, and You will hear and save."

**No Fear**

I love the effect of God's presence. When He shows up, fear has to leave. When you hear the back door slam—that's fear leaving. When worry vacates the premises, His presence brings "fullness of joy" and "pleasures forevermore" (Psalm 16:11). When passing the torch of national leadership to Joshua, Moses reminded him, "The Lord, He is the One who goes before you.

He will be with you, He will not leave you nor forsake you; do not fear nor be dismayed" (Deuteronomy 31:8).

Aren't you glad that God goes before you? Aren't you glad that He is in the "storm" before the storm reaches you? He will not leave you nor forsake you. Do not fear nor be dismayed.

Wherever His presence is...there we will find His peace and love (Isaiah 26:3). "You will keep Him in perfect peace, whose mind is stayed on You, because he trusts in You." His love will overshadow our worries. The apostle John writes:

> *There is no fear in love; but perfect love casts out fear, because fear involves torment. But he who fears has not been made perfect in love. We love Him because He first loved us.* 1 John 4:18

# CHAPTER SEVEN

# Survival Principle 3:

## KNOW TO WHOM YOU BELONG

When Paul told his shipmates about the angel who had appeared to him, he described this angel as a representative of "the God to whom I belong and whom I serve" (Acts 27:23).

In essence, Paul was saying, "Let me tell you which God this is. He's not one of the gods you Greeks worship, but He's Yahweh, the King of kings and the Lord of lords.

Knowing to Whom we belong is like having a compass in our survival kit. The compass keeps us pointed in the right direction. It keeps us on track. If you don't know who you are serving or who you belong to, you're going to have trouble getting through the "storm" in your life. You'll become lost without a sense of direction.

## Belonging to God

Paul described his God as the one "to whom I belong" (Acts 27:23). As Christians, we are God's property. In fact, from God's perspective, we are seated; we've already been delivered; and are now enjoying the victory. God has "raised us up together, and made us sit together in the heavenly places in Christ Jesus" (Ephesians 2:6). Paul in effect said, "I am seated. I am in a place of rest despite the storm."

It was only through faith in Christ that Paul could declare this.

Jesus grants you and I the right to be called children of God. John 1:12-13 says, "As many as received Him, to them He gave the right to become children of God, to those who believe in His name: who were born, not of blood, nor of the will of the flesh, nor of the will of man, but of God."

If God has granted me the right to be born again, to be born into His kingdom, nobody can reverse that. "If God is for us, who can be against us?" (Romans 8:31). We belong to Him. Therefore, we reside in Him.

**Serving God**

Paul declared, "This is where my confidence lies; this is where I belong: in God." Then he said that this was not only the God "to whom I belong" but also the God "whom I serve" (Acts 27:23). Interestingly, the Greek word for "serve" here can also be translated "worship."

When the storms of life come, we turn in the direction of that which we worship, don't we? If you want to know what people are like, watch them in the midst of a trial, because who they really are will surface. The storm blows away the spiritual facade and the phoniness and exposes what is really there. Paul wrote in Romans 6:16-18,

> *Do you not know that to whom you present yourselves slaves to obey, you are that one's slaves whom you obey, whether of sin leading to death, or of obedience leading to righteousness? But God be thanked that though you were slaves of sin, yet*

*you obeyed from the heart that form of doctrine to which you were delivered. And having been set free from sin, you became slaves of righteousness.*

The "storm" will reveal to any of us what we're bound to. "Am I enslaved to the righteousness of God, or am I enslaved to something else?" That's what a "storm" will reveal to us. Storms have a way of reminding us of who we serve. The winds of turmoil and trails drive us back to the haven of our true devotion. David said, "It is good for me that I have been afflicted" (Psalm 119:71). Why? Because it brought me back to my *first love,* to the One worthy of my service.

**Knowing God Now**
Paul belonged to the Lord and was serving the Lord long before the storm came. The key to making it through a "storm" is to belong to Him now and serve Him now, before the "storm" gets here.

What a lot of people do is like jumping out of an airplane at thirty thousand feet and trying to put on a parachute as they are falling to the ground. It can be intimidating to see the ground drawing closer and closer while trying to remember all the instructions on how to put on a parachute. Wouldn't it be better to put the parachute on while you're in the plane? Then, when you're free-falling, you just pull the cord and the parachute opens.

I've known people who never show up for church when things are going well, but let them go through a crisis, and they are there every week. They are the first ones to come in on Sunday, Wednesday night, anytime the doors are open. But as soon as the crisis is past, you don't see them anymore.

Why not serve God before the storm comes, so that when the "storm" hits, you're ready to go through it because you already belong to Him and you already are serving Him? God wants us to consistently follow Him, starting before the "storm" comes, so that we can make it through.

# CHAPTER EIGHT

# Survival Principle 4:

PRAY FOR YOURSELF AND FOR OTHERS

When the angel spoke to Paul on the ship, he said, "Do not be afraid, Paul; you must be brought before Caesar; and indeed God has granted you all those who sail with you" (Acts 27:24).

"Granted"? What does that mean? It means that Paul had been requesting their safety in prayer. All the time when it seemed like Paul was not doing anything, he was actually praying for God to spare him and all those on board.

This gives us our fourth survival principle. We must pray, not only for ourselves, but for others as well.

## Praying for Enemies

To me, there is nothing very surprising about Paul praying during the storm. What *is* amazing, however, is that Paul was praying, not only for himself and his companions Luke and Aristarchus, but also for his enemies. He was praying for his jailer, the centurion, as well as for the helmsman and ship owner, all three of whom had made the foolish decision that got him into the situation where he found himself: tossed about in a frightening storm.

The "storms" we face are often caused, at least in part, by other people. We go through struggles because of choices made by our spouse, our co-workers, or people in our church. But it's still our responsibility to pray for them (Matthew 5:44).

How many of us are willing to pray for those people who have put us in the tough situation we are going through? Paul did. He was not pouting; he was praying.

The quickest way to overcome unforgiveness within ourselves is to pray for those who have offended us. This, of course, should not be a token prayer like

"Lord, change my husband" or "God, just do something with this person who has hurt me." That's not praying; that's complaining. When I talk about praying for enemies, I mean praying until your heart weeps for your enemies the way Jesus wept for you.

Paul had been *beseeching* God in prayer, probably even weeping over the lives of those with him in the storm.

Do you pray for people that way? Have you wept over people who have offended you? Or have you sacrificed them on the altar of bitterness and hatred?

**The Root and Fruit of Bitterness**
The right kind of prayer is important because it keeps us from having a heart of bitterness. I don't care how popular you are, what your ministry is, or how rich you are—God cannot use you or keep you if you are bitter.

Hebrews 12:14–15 urges, "Pursue peace with all people...looking carefully...lest any root of bitterness springing up cause trouble."

God wants you to stay away from bitterness because it stinks up the temple of your heart. It stinks up your family; it stinks up your job; it stinks up your life. In fact, it defiles everything it comes in contact with.

Unforgiveness breeds spiritual stagnation within a church and within an individual's life. But long before the hardening of our wills to forgive other people, there is a hardening of our hearts toward God. When we harden our heart and say, "I just can't forgive that person," we've hardened our heart against God. We've forgotten that we are to extend the same grace toward others that He has extended toward us.

Ephesians 4:32 says, "Be kind to one another, tenderhearted, forgiving one another, even as God in Christ forgave you." How has God in Christ forgiven you? He has forgiven you *unconditionally.* What does that mean? Unconditional forgiveness can't be earned, and we don't deserve it. But God has unconditionally forgiven us. And we are to forgive other people in the same way.

Many people will protest and say, "But you don't know what they've done to me, Pastor. If you were in my shoes, you would understand."

No, I don't know. But God knows. And more than that, God knows what you have done to His Son.

Because of you, His Son was beaten, was nailed to a cross, and died. And yet, knowing all that would happen, He still sent Jesus. Bloody and beaten, the thorns pressed into His brow, this Savior looked down from the cross and said, "Father, forgive them, for they do not know what they do" (Luke 23:34). And so now the Father says, "The same way that My Son has forgiven you, you need to forgive other people who have offended you."

### "I'm Offended!"

One of the problems in the church is that there are too many people walking around feeling offended. When someone says or does something that offends us, we run off to another church. It's no longer a question of attending a church where we feel God has called us. We have been offended.

Thus, without the leading of the Holy Spirit, we've decided to attend another fellowship, only to repeat the process all over again.

Where does such an attitude come from? If we're honest, it comes from the very pit of hell!

How can anyone who is dead be offended? The Bible says we have died in Christ. "I have been crucified with Christ; it is no longer I who live, but Christ lives in me; and the life which I now live in the flesh I live by faith in the Son of God, who loved me and gave Himself for me" (Galatians 2:20). How can we be offended and hold a grudge unless we are still alive?

Now, we do have feelings, and people say and do things that hurt our feelings. We may feel offended, but we can't walk around carrying that offense in our hearts. We must *choose* to forgive immediately. Offenses will come, but as surely as the offense comes, God will supply the grace we need to forgive.

It's important for us to remember that, as we're going through a "storm," we should pray for others, especially for those who have offended us. In doing so, we will find that God will set us free from the bondage of bitterness, even while we are going through the storm.

# Survival Principle 5:

BOLDLY DECLARE YOUR FAITH

Sometimes when we're going through a storm, the last thing we want to do is testify to our faith in Jesus Christ. However, that's what Paul did. He declared, "Take heart, men, for I believe God that it will be just as it was told me" (Acts 27:25). He did not wait to proclaim his belief when the sun came out and the sea grew calm.

Paul was still in the middle of the storm. The boat was being tossed back and forth; the sky was dark; the passengers were having a hard time holding on. In the midst of the hopelessness, Paul stood up and gave a testimony of faith.

If the presence of God is like a life preserver in a survival kit, and if knowing to whom you belong is like a compass in the kit, then declaring your faith is like food in that survival kit. Paul declared his faith, and faith has to do with the Word of God, and God's Word is what satisfies and sustains the soul.

**Standing Up**

Our declaration of faith can be food for ourselves as well as for others who hear it. When we are in the midst of a storm, we can stand up and proclaim our belief that God is going to take care of us. We can stand upon what God has said to us. People need to see believers standing up in the boat.

We live in a time of great wickedness. The daily events reported in the media can cause us to say, "It's a lost cause. I might as well sit here and not do anything but wait for Jesus to come back." But then God speaks to our heart: "Get your eyes off what the devil is doing, and get your eyes on what I am doing, because greater is He who is in you than he who is in the world" (see 1 John 4:4). Where sin abounds, grace abounds the more (Romans 5:20).

## Take Action—Get Involved

In a world full of much trouble and pain, what can one person do? We can get involved in what God is doing, find out where He's moving and get involved. No matter how hopeless it is around us, no matter how much despair is around us, we can stand up and proclaim God's Word.

In fact, the greatest time to declare what we believe is in the midst of the "storm." Why? Because faith is contagious. People are drawn to others who stand by faith. Paul was among the hopeless and the dying when he declared his confidence in what God had spoken to him. That's when we need to stand up too, now more than ever.

## Telling the Truth

Notice that Paul was not telling the men on board ship his opinion, but only what God had spoken to him.

People who are in a storm don't want sensationalism; they want the truth. They don't care if you know how to tap-dance or sing well or play an instrument; they want the truth. They don't want false hope; they want the truth. They don't want to have their ears tickled; they want the truth. The truth is able to set them free.

And not only that but also the truth sustains our soul. If God sustains us, then we're able to minister to other people by His Word in the midst of the storm. Consider the words of Jeremiah 15:16:

> *Your words were found, and I ate them,*
> *And Your word was to me the joy and*
> *rejoicing of my heart;*
> *For I am called by Your name,*
> *O LORD God of hosts.*

What was Paul rejoicing over? Some religious formula of confession? No. He was rejoicing over what God had spoken to him. That's what we rejoice over in the storm—the Word of God.

# CHAPTER TEN

# Survival Plan

If you're going to make it through the storms of your life, you need a survival plan:

1. Jettison excess weight.
2. Remember that God is with you.
3. Know to whom you belong.
4. Pray for yourself and others.
5. Boldly declare your faith.

**Be Prepared**

How can you maintain your survival plan? Jeremiah 29:11-13 says, "I know the thoughts that I think toward you, says the LORD, thoughts of peace and not of evil, to give you a future and a hope. Then you will call upon Me and go and pray to Me, and I will listen to you. And you will seek Me and find Me, when you search for Me with all your heart." We can seek and find Him even in the midst of our storms if we have been searching for Him with all our hearts.

God has prepared a future and a hope for us, but we must also be spiritually prepared to walk in our destinies.

There is no storm that can derail us from God's plan and purpose for our lives. However, the believer who fails to seek God daily will not be prepared for the storm. When storms come, the unprepared Christian will easily be blown off God's course for his or her life by the winds of the storm.

If we will seek God first, He will compensate our weakness with His grace, even in the time of great turmoil. He knows we are human.

Paul learned a lesson about strength and weakness. Jesus told him, "My grace is sufficient for you, for My strength is made perfect in weakness" (2 Corinthians 12:9).

God's grace is sufficient for us even when we're going through a "storm." We may not be strong in ourselves, but our weakness can be exchanged for His strength.

# Part 3

---

## Blessings in the Storm

## Part 3
## Blessings in the Storm

*Now when the fourteenth night had come,
as we were driven up and down in the
Adriatic Sea, about midnight the sailors
sensed that they were drawing near some
land. And they took soundings and found it
to be twenty fathoms; and when they had
gone a little farther, they took soundings
again and found it to be fifteen fathoms.
Then, fearing lest we should run aground on
the rocks, they dropped four anchors from
the stern, and prayed for day to come. And
as the sailors were seeking to escape from
the ship, when they had let down the skiff
into the sea, under pretense of putting out
anchors from the prow, Paul said to the centurion and the soldiers, "Unless these men
stay in the ship, you cannot be saved."
Then the soldiers cut away the ropes of the
skiff and let it fall off.*

*And as day was about to dawn, Paul
implored them all to take food, saying,
"Today is the fourteenth day you have waited and continued without food, and eaten*

*nothing. Therefore I urge you to take nourishment, for this is for your survival, since not a hair will fall from the head of any of you." And when he had said these things, he took bread and gave thanks to God in the presence of them all; and when he had broken it he began to eat. Then they were all encouraged, and also took food themselves. And in all we were two hundred and seventy-six persons on the ship. So when they had eaten enough, they lightened the ship and threw out the wheat into the sea.*

*When it was day, they did not recognize the land; but they observed a bay with a beach, onto which they planned to run the ship if possible. And they let go the anchors and left them in the sea, meanwhile loosing the rudder ropes; and they hoisted the mainsail to the wind and made for shore. But striking a place where two seas met, they ran the ship aground; and the prow stuck fast and remained immovable, but the stern was being broken up by the violence of the waves.*

*And the soldiers' plan was to kill the prison-
ers, lest any of them should swim away and
escape. But the centurion, wanting to save
Paul, kept them from their purpose, and
commanded that those who could swim
should jump overboard first and get to land,
and the rest, some on boards and some on
parts of the ship. And so it was that they all
escaped safely to land.*

—Acts 27:27-44

# CHAPTER ELEVEN

# Blessing 1: Commitment

I remember my mom giving me cod liver oil when I was a kid. Sometimes I'd get an orange juice chaser, but other times she would just say, "Here, boy, open your mouth...this is good for you."

Mom said it was good for me. However, I remember thinking, *Man, how can something so bad be good?* But indeed, Mom knew what she was talking about.

We all go through things in life that are not pleasant but are indeed good for us.

As I think about the blessings that can come from the "storms" in my life, I'm reminded of Psalm 119:71:

*It is good for me that I have been afflicted, that I may learn your statutes.*

It's good to be afflicted? David sounds like a sadist here, but he has come to see the benefit of trials from God's perspective. God looks at "storms" differently than we do. Like mothers who give their children cod liver oil, He knows what's best for us. He knows that the awful, temporary taste will result in our personal health and well-being.

### Three Blessings in Paul's Storm

There are three blessings that emerge from Paul's experience in the storm. These blessings are also applicable to our own trials. The first blessing is one of "commitment." The second has to do with "hunger;" the third has to do with "brokenness."

### Commitment

God brought everyone on board the ship to a point of commitment. He brought them to a point where they would trust God or perish.

After being driven back and forth at the mercy of the wind, the sailors began to sense that they might be nearing land. To make sure, they lowered a weight and discovered that indeed the bottom was only twenty fathoms (120 feet) deep. When they had gone a little farther, they took soundings again and found the bottom to be fifteen fathoms (90 feet) below them.

Afraid that the ship would wreck on some rocks, the sailors lowered four anchors from the rear of the ship, attempting to slow their progress. Then they waited, hoping daylight would come soon so they could see where they were. It seemed to be the only thing they could do. Or was it?

### An Escape Attempt Foiled

Some of the sailors were not prepared to wait but hatched a plan to escape from the ship. They went to the front of the ship, pretending to set out anchors from that point. Their real intention was to lower the skiff, or lifeboat, into the water and escape. They were going to abandon the other travelers and try to make it safely to shore on their own.

Paul saw what was going on and said to the soldiers, "Unless these men stay in the ship, you cannot be saved" (Acts 27:31). The Greek word Paul used here for "you" is *humeis,* which means "yourselves." In other words, Paul was not saying that the escaping sailors would not be saved; he was saying that the whole ship's company would perish. The men who would best know how to run the ship safely aground (assuming that it was possible) were trying to leave. If they were allowed to leave, it would place the ship in a bad situation.

The soldiers believed Paul and cut the lines, setting the skiff adrift.

Can you imagine the looks on the sailors' faces when their lifeboat disappeared into the gloom of night? They must have been thinking, *That was our only hope.* But through this desperate measure they had been brought to a place of true commitment, whether they wanted to be there or not.

### Losing the Lifeboat

As we learned previously, the sailors had already jettisoned nearly everything they could from the ship, including the ship's tackle (Acts 27:18-19). But for many days they still had the lifeboat firmly lashed to the deck. They were not yet completely committed.

In the same way, God sometimes has to come in and cut off that which we feel is our only hope. He removes something that we have been trusting in, so as to get us to completely commit ourselves to Him.

Halfhearted commitments produce fair-weather friends. People will say, "I'm with you, brother." You think they are dropping anchors and preparing to stay with you in the ship throughout the storm, but really they are putting out the skiff. They are not committed. In case of emergency, they will step into the lifeboat and say, "See you later."

The same thing can happen in a marriage or any other relationship that requires commitment. Some people seem prepared to stick it out, while all along they are working on their exit strategy.

In the Old Testament, many of the ancient kings of Judah and Israel were committed to God, but not wholeheartedly. For example, the Bible declares, "Asa did what was right in the eyes of the Lord" (1 Kings 15:11). Then comes the footnote: "But the high places were not removed" (verse 14). The high places were mounds or hills where other gods were worshiped. So while Asa basically followed the one true God, he was not faithful to obey God by eliminating pagan worship from the land. He was not fully committed.

A lot of believers have thrown the "tackle" overboard—they're showing up for church and saying and doing all the right things. But they still have a "lifeboat" attached...a plan of escape. This plan is according to their own wisdom. It is a "just in case" plan, should the storm become too severe and beyond their ability to endure.

Many so-called believers are lowering the lifeboat instead of the anchor. What are you lowering today?

Are you lowering the anchor? Are you anchored in Jesus Christ? Are you fully committed to the gospel of Jesus Christ?

Or are you lowering the lifeboat? Are you planning your exit in the skiff of compromise?

God will not let us get away with giving only 99.9 percent. He wants it all. He wants us to put our trust in Him completely.

God is our Jehovah Raah, which means "The Lord is my shepherd." David knew this and said, "I shall not want" (Psalm 23:1). If we've got God as our Shepherd looking after our soul, then we will not lack anything we really need.

God is also our refuge and our strength. Psalm 121 says this:

*I will lift up my eyes to the hills—*
*From whence comes my help?*
*My help comes from the LORD,*
*Who made heaven and earth.*
*He will not allow your foot to be moved;*
*He who keeps you will not slumber.*
*Behold, He who keeps Israel*
*Shall neither slumber nor sleep.*
*The LORD is your keeper;*
*The LORD is your shade at your right hand.*
*The sun shall not strike you by day,*
*Nor the moon by night.*
*The LORD shall preserve you from all evil;*
*He shall preserve your soul.*

*The LORD shall preserve your going out and your coming in*
*From this time forth, and even forevermore.*

Oh, I could tell you stories about how God has been my deliverer. And I am sure you could tell how God has been your deliverer as well. The storm is often God's way of getting rid of all of our other options so that we *have* to trust God, and God alone, to rescue us.

## The Problem with Options

One of the problems with our lifestyle in America is that we have far too many options.

Do you need to buy a vehicle? Well, do you want a sedan, a sports car, an SUV, or a minivan? New or used? What model? What color? What options do you desire?

God wants us to get rid of all options but Him. One of the blessings of the storm is that God cuts away our skiffs. It may not seem like a blessing at the time—in fact, it might scare us silly. But it really is for the best. Only then can we truly find the eye of the storm, the power of God within which surpasses all understanding, enabling us to endure the storm without.

> *Trust in the LORD with all your heart, and lean not on your own understanding; in all your ways acknowledge Him, and He shall direct your paths.* Proverbs 3:5–6

# CHAPTER TWELVE

# Blessing 2: Hunger

In a previous chapter, I mentioned the movie character Rocky. Do you remember the part in the *Rocky* movie series where the boxer loses his hunger for winning? He gets fat and lazy, and then he gets his "clock cleaned" (knocked out in a boxing match) because he has lost his edge.

God expects us to maintain a spiritual hunger and pursue Him. The psalmist declared,

*As the deer pants for the water brooks,*
*So pants my soul for You, O God.*
Psalm 42:1

Why is the deer panting? He's thirsty. And for us to truly follow God, we've got to be hungry and thirsty for Him. This is the second and unexpected blessing in the storm: spiritual hunger.

## Breakfast at Sea

The sailors had not eaten for the duration of the storm. Maybe they were fasting to appease their gods. Or maybe they had just lost their appetites after being tossed to and fro so violently by the storm.

In any case, Paul told them, "I urge you to take nourishment, for this is for your survival, since not a hair will fall from the head of any of you" (Acts 27:34). Then he set the example for them. He gave thanks to God and started to eat. Because of this, the sailors "were all encouraged, and also took food themselves" (verse 36).

After eating, the ship's crew did a remarkable thing. Up to this point, they had left the ship's cargo of grain alone, even though they had lightened the ship of other sources of weight. But now they threw all of this valuable cargo of grain overboard. Now the ship was ready for what was about to come.

**Appetite for Life**

We should note that Paul encouraged the others to take nourishment "for your survival" (Acts 27:34).

The sailors had lost their appetite for life. If you had asked one of them, in the midst of the storm, if he wanted to eat some bread, he probably would have answered: "Eat bread? Why? We're going to be dead tomorrow. Why should I give nourishment to a body that's about to be destroyed?"

Many today know that feeling. They're not in danger of drowning, but they don't have a reason for living. They dread getting out of bed in the morning. They have no hope, no appetite for life.

This is not how God wants us to live. Jesus said, "I have come that they may have life, and that they may have it more abundantly" (John 10:10). He wants us to have an appetite for living.

**Encouragement through Action**

To the hopeless sailors, Paul provided encouragement by his actions. As in a traditional Jewish home, Paul took the bread, offered a blessing to God, and ate. The others watched what he was doing and joined him in eating.

This shows us the power of our witness through action. It is true that in the midst of crisis situations we need to speak words of faith. But then we also need to follow up our words with actions.

Eating the bread was an act of faith on Paul's part. Jesus is the bread of life (John 6:35). As we turn to Him and trust in Him and make Him the center of our lives, people see our actions and are encouraged. In Paul's case, he broke physical bread and ate it. As a result, the sailors "were all encouraged" (Acts 27:36).

Why were these weary, hungry, and probably dehydrated men encouraged by Paul's actions? By virtue of the fact that he was eating the bread, he was saying to them, "There is a reason to live for tomorrow." He assured them, "Not a hair will fall from the head of any of you" (verse 34). They were really beginning to believe Paul's message that they would live and not die.

Isn't that the gospel? When people are hopeless, have no reason to live, and come to the end of themselves, they are hungry for something, even though they don't know what it is. In such a moment, believers can come to them and offer them the bread of eternal life, which is the gospel of Jesus Christ. Thus they are imparting to others the "true life," giving them a reason to live. Only through Christ the Bread of Life will they begin to believe the message that we preach—that they will live and not die.

**Full of God**

The sailors could throw away the wheat because they had already eaten their fill.

Let's say you're going out to a restaurant to eat. I'm not talking about hamburger and French fries; I'm talking about a three-course meal with all the trimmings. You eat and eat. You even order dessert. As you are getting up from the table, you think, *I shouldn't have eaten so much, but oh, it was so good.*

If someone were to come up to you at just that moment and offer you a prime rib, would you want it? Of course not! You're already full, and the prime rib wouldn't even look appealing.

It's the same way with spiritual things. When we are full of God, the morsels of the world do not attract us any longer. When we are gorged on God's goodness, we are no longer hungry for the things that don't really satisfy.

The devil comes and says, "Hey, how about this?"

It is our responsibility to say, "No thanks. I'm full. I'm full of the Holy Spirit. I'm full of God's power. I'm full of God. There's no room in my life for compromise, because I'm full."

On the other hand, carnal cravings can overcome us when we have lost our appetite for God. That's why we are exhorted in Scripture to seek God more and more.

The author of the letter to the Hebrews said to his readers, "Though by this time you ought to be teachers, you need someone to teach you again the first principles of the oracles of God; and you have come to need milk and not solid food" (Hebrews 5:12). It's a rebuke. He was saying, "Grow up! You've been feeding on the junk food of society and not on the nourishment of God's Word, and you're not maturing in Him."

When we keep feeding on the solid food of God's Word, we will be satisfied in Him and safe from the deceitfulness of sin.

The spiritual nourishment we need doesn't cost us anything. God freely gives spiritual food to us. Isaiah 55:1-2 says,

> *Ho! Everyone who thirsts,*
> *Come to the waters;*
> *And you who have no money,*
> *Come, buy and eat.*
> *Yes, come, buy wine and milk*
> *Without money and without price.*
> *Why do you spend money for what is*
> *not bread,*
> *And your wages for what does not satisfy?*
> *Listen carefully to Me, and eat what is good,*
> *And let your soul delight itself in abundance.*

God wants us to delight ourselves in His abundance. In other words, God wants us to be gorged on His goodness.

A new wardrobe won't do it. Only Jesus can fill the void within our lives.

## Real Bread

Not long ago, a famous recording artist suffered an emotional breakdown and was under psychiatric care. From the world's perspective, this famous female artist had everything: Talent. Wealth. Fame. So what happened? Spiritually speaking, she was on the wrong diet, one that could never satisfy her soul.

Are you spending your life on that which is not bread?

Maybe you've lost your appetite for the things of God. God may be sending a "storm" your way to create a hunger in you once again for the things of God.

And once He creates a hunger in us—that hunger can prove to be a beautiful thing—then He comes along and fills it. He fills that emptiness with Him until we're overflowing with His goodness.

God is a good God. He has not come to condemn you but so that you might have life in Him (John 3:16-17).

# Blessing 3: Brokenness

The last blessing in the storm is broken-ness. Brokenness is of great importance to God, but if we are honest, it is not at the top of our list.

When was the last time you received a flyer in the mail advertising a seminar on brokenness with the invitation "Come spend three days with us and be broken"?

We will readily sign up for a free semi-nar on how to be blessed, but we will go out of our way to avoid one titled "Brokenness."

God wants us to be blessed, but the thing we often forget is that there is a *blessedness* in *brokenness*.

## Shipwreck

The dawn revealed to the weary travelers that they were nearing land. It was the island of Malta, though they did not recognize it as such at the time. Trying to control the ship with anchors and sails, they headed for a beach, hoping for a soft landing.

The drama of this voyage had one final act. The ship was caught in two currents, with its front end now stuck fast in the ground. The waves, meanwhile, began to tear the ship apart.

In a desperate move the soldiers decided to kill the prisoners. They were responsible for the prisoners and would have to pay dearly with their lives if the prisoners escaped. The centurion overruled the soldiers because he desired to save Paul.

The centurion issued new orders. All who could swim were to jump overboard first and head for land. The others were to make their way to shore as best they could, by way of the debris adrift from the ship.

Remarkably, every person on board—some two hundred seventy-six men (Acts 27:37)—made it safely to shore. The ship, however, was destroyed.

**Two Seas**

They had planned to run aground some place along the beach, which appeared to be a safe place to guide the ship. When they tried, they ran into two seas, which then forced them to run aground.

Spiritually speaking, it's usually at a place where two "seas" meet that the "ship of our will" is broken up. Joshua said, "Choose for yourselves this day whom you will serve" (Joshua 24:15). We can't serve God and self; we can't have two masters.

God often brings us to a place of brokenness through a crisis in which we have to make a decision about whether we're going to obey God or obey the dictates of the world or our flesh. Like the ship meeting the two seas, something has to give.

**For the Glory of God**

In the aftermath of a "storm," God often delivers us to safety on the fragments of our own brokenness. God will break up the very thing we used to trust in.

In Paul's case, God caused the ship to run aground, and then began to break into pieces.

After everyone was saved, God did not want the sailors to rejoice because of their abilities or because of the strength of the vessel. God wanted them to rejoice in the God whom Paul belonged to and served.

That's why God sends brokenness into our lives—so that He might be glorified. We don't always arrive at our destinations the way we want to, but we can get there according to our faith in Christ and by His grace.

## Using the Broken

There's another reason God allows brokenness in our lives: because God can only use people who have been broken.

God cannot use the proud. If we will humble ourselves under the mighty hand of God, He will lift us up and use us for His glory.

Someone once wrote that God uses for His glory those people and things that are the most perfectly broken. They are the sacrifices in which He delights. Here are some examples of how God uses that which is broken:

- It was through the breaking down of Jacob's natural strength at Peniel that he was brought to the place where God could clothe him with spiritual power (Genesis 32:22-32).

- It was the breaking of the rock at Horeb by the striking of Moses' rod that let the cool water flow to the thirsty people of Israel (Exodus 17:1-7).

- It was when the three hundred elect soldiers under Gideon broke their pitchers (which is a type of breaking of ourselves) that the hidden light shone forth to the consternation of their adversaries (Judges 7:15-22).

- It was when the poor widow broke the seal of the little pot of oil and poured it forth that God multiplied it to pay all her debts and to supply a means of her support (2 Kings 4:1-7).

- It was when Jesus took the five loaves and broke them that the bread was multiplied sufficiently to feed five thousand men (Matthew 14:13-21).

- It was when Mary broke her beautiful alabaster box of ointment that the pent-up perfume filled the house (Matthew 26:6-13).

- And so, too, when Jesus allowed His precious body to be broken by the thorns, the nails, and the spear, redemption poured forth like a crystal stream from which sinners could drink and live (1 Corinthians 11:24).

Yes, God blesses and uses broken things. David said in Psalm 51:17,

*The sacrifices of God are a broken spirit,*
*A broken and a contrite heart—*
*These, O God, You will not despise.*

Are you broken? Then rejoice! For where our strength ends, His begins, and He is able to deliver you through the storms.

## A Shipwreck of Egos

God sent brokenness to the sailors, the soldiers, and the prisoners. Yet through their brokenness He delivered them safely to land. God sends brokenness to us in the same way. He uses a "storm" to demolish our egos.

As the vessels of Gideon and the three hundred were broken (Judges 7), the light shone forth. We must be broken before the light of God can shine forth from us. The light of our egos must decrease, that the light of the Son might shine through:

> *For we who live are always delivered to death for Jesus' sake, that the life of Jesus also may be manifested in our mortal flesh.* 2 Corinthians 4:11

# CHAPTER FOURTEEN

# Things to Remember

We have learned a lot about weathering the "storms" in our life throughout this book. By way of conclusion, I want to leave you with a few comments. They may help you with your perspective on what God is doing in your life.

## 1. Life Is Supposed to Be a Grid, Not a Grind.

We had an artist paint a mural for our church. Out of curiosity, I questioned him about the process used to paint a mural. Being uninformed about it, I thought you simply start painting. However, I learned that if you do that, one part of the picture will not match up with another on the mural. The artist revealed the secret of how to keep the mural artistically correct.

"Before I start painting, I draw a grid on the wall. All the great artists drew and painted on grids."

As I watched, the mural artist sectioned off the wall and painted one section at a time. The mural came out beautifully, with all the pieces matching up.

I find that it is helpful to look at our lives as a large grid made up of many sections. Many times we can't understand what God is doing, and that's because we're looking at only one square in the grid. Maybe that part of the grid is filled with trouble—a storm. We become obsessed with what is going on in that part of our grid and think that's all there is to our life. We may even get discouraged and think life is over.

But God says, "That's just one part of the grid! I've got a whole mural that I'm painting for your life."

Life is a grid, not a grind. Sometimes when we focus on just one part of the grid, we begin to feel like we're in a grind. If you don't like your job, for example, you might keep thinking, *Oh man, I've got to get up and go to work tomorrow.* You're dragging along and getting discouraged because you're focused on just one part of the grid. Your life, however, is more than the job you have right now.

What sort of picture is God painting of your life? The Bible says that the model He is looking at is in heaven, because He is looking at Jesus and then He's painting on you.

The Bible says, "It has not yet been revealed what we shall be, but we know that when He is revealed, we shall be like Him, for we shall see Him as He is" (1 John 3:2). Hallelujah! God is making you like His Son, and He's doing it by painting one grid at a time.

When something bad happens in your life, tell yourself that the trouble is just one part of the entire grid. And say to God, "I don't understand what this means, Lord. I can't figure it out. But you have the big picture. Nevertheless, the end result will be that I will be like Jesus."

All He asks us to do is to trust Him. Leave the brush in His hand. Don't take it out and say, "I want to be painted like this." That's when we get into trouble. Our life is not a grind; it is a grid.

## 2. Not All Storms Are Bad.

A storm is an opportunity to glorify God. The apostle Peter wrote this:

> *Beloved, do not think it strange concerning the fiery trial which is to try you, as though some strange thing happened to you; but rejoice to the extent that you partake of Christ's sufferings, that when His glory is revealed, you may also be glad with exceeding joy. If you are reproached for the name of Christ, blessed are you, for the Spirit of glory and of God rests upon you. On their part He is blasphemed, but on your part He is glorified. But let none of you suffer as a murderer, a thief, an evildoer, or as a busybody in other people's matters. Yet if anyone suffers as a Christian, let him not be ashamed, but let him glorify God in this matter.*

*For the time has come for judgment to begin at the house of God; and if it begins with us first, what will be the end of those who do not obey the gospel of God?*

*Now "If the righteous one is scarcely saved, where will the ungodly and the sinner appear?"*

*Therefore let those who suffer according to the will of God commit their souls to Him in doing good, as to a faithful Creator.* 1 Peter 4:12-19

The point Peter makes in the above verses is, regardless of the situation you find yourself in, give God glory.

I had a brother walk up to me one Wednesday night after our time of prayer and say, "You know what it all boils down to, Pastor? It's a question of, 'will I give Him glory?'" At the time, this brother was going through a separation from his wife and some other difficult things. He said, "God told me to not be fretting about all these things. God just asked me if I would give Him glory? That's what it really boils down to."

He's right. Life boils down to whether we will give God glory.

Paul, in the midst of the raging sea, decided to give God glory. By virtue of his faith, lives were saved.

Job said, "Though He slay me, yet will I trust Him" (Job 13:15). He was willing to trust God even if God took his life without giving him a reason.

My prayer is "Lord, give *me* that kind of faith." I don't want wishy-washy, on-again, off-again Christianity. I'm tired of it. It makes me sick. I want to go all the way with God. God says, "I could wish you were cold or hot" (Revelation 3:15). He doesn't have time for lukewarm people.

How far will you trust God? Will you trust Him only if He gives you everything you want? Will you trust Him even if everything goes wrong? Glorify God no matter what. Glorify Him even in your "storm."

### 3. We Shouldn't Underestimate Our Faithfulness toward God.

Through Paul's faithfulness, people who once felt condemned to die were saved.

Somebody's watching your life today. They may not say, "I'm watching you," but they're watching you.

Sometimes I feel like the devil is beating up on me. I think, *That's it! I'm going to quit. I'm going to get another job and run away from my troubles.*

Then I remember the church, and little kids will grab me by the leg and say, "Pastor Al! Pastor Al!" "How are you doing, Pastor Al?" "Look at this, Pastor Al."

Then I have to pray, "Lord, my faithfulness to what You called me to do is going to touch these kids. I'm not just going to touch these people in the church; I'm going to touch generations. What can I do but obey You?"

Somebody's watching you. Your grandkids, your children, your co-workers, etc. And your faithfulness in the storm will affect their lives. It may even save them as it saved the condemned men Paul encountered on this doomed vessel.

121

## 4. God Uses Storms to Elevate the Believer and Subjugate the World.

Notice that Paul was in charge during the storm. Before the storm came, Paul was a nobody. But when the storm came, faith suddenly elevated him, and those of the world became subjugated to him. The world was brought low and Paul was lifted high.

God uses storms to elevate our faith. The best time for a Christian to witness is in the midst of the storm. God exalts us by the power of His Holy Spirit. Psalm 37:34 says,

*Wait on the LORD,*
*And keep His way,*
*And He shall exalt you to inherit the land;*
*When the wicked are cut off, you shall see it.*

When we stand up in the storm, the world takes notice, because faith takes precedence over the natural and the assaults of the logic of man. When we stand in faith as Paul stood in faith on the ship in the storm, we stand in the authority of God's Word. Thus the

Word of faith exalts us above the storm, through the power of God, enabling us to be witnesses to others in the storm.

## 5. God Knows Our Limits.

Many years ago the British Parliament passed a law requiring that all British ships display a load line called the Plimsoll mark. It indicates the maximum depth a vessel can be submerged in the water without danger during a storm. This regulation, named for the reformer Samuel Plimsoll, has prevented many disasters at sea and saved thousands of lives. Because of this, Plimsoll became known as "the Sailors' Friend."

In the same way, God knows where the Plimsoll mark is within our own lives. Therefore, the temptations and trials He allows to come our way will never exceed our capacity to bear them. Why? Because He knows our limits.

I'm glad God knows what I can bear. First Corinthians 10:13 says, "No temptation has overtaken you except such as is common to man; but God is faithful, who will not allow you to be tempted beyond what you are able, but with the temptation will also make the way of escape, that you may be able to bear it."

God enabled those sailors and prisoners and soldiers to escape to safety. He understood what they were able to bear. He understands what we are able to bear as well.

Remember this: when storms come, we can be of good cheer. Why? Because our Father is always near. His hand is gently reinforcing our commitment to Him. His hand is creating a hunger in us for His righteousness. And His hand is delivering us to a place of brokenness so that we might see His glory revealed in us.

Commitment, hunger, brokenness—these are important to God and they should be important to us as well.

Although "storms" come into our lives, never for a second will they alter God's plan for our lives. Remember that!

Paul must have had mixed emotions when it looked as if they were all destined for a watery grave at the bottom of that sea. Yet God did a great work.

Paul didn't know exactly how God would help them; he only knew there would be no loss of life. God proved faithful and true to His Word.

When Paul crawled up onto the shore of Malta, the Lord was not through with him. God even performed great miracles through Paul, the apostle of Malta! Perhaps God orchestrated the storm for the sake of those souls on the island who heard and believed on the gospel. Great blessings and good came out of Paul's difficulties and trials.

King David saw the glory of God through the many trials he faced in His life. Chosen by God as King of Israel, he still faced severe storms. We can all take to heart the words of David's triumphant psalm as he declares:

*Though an army may encamp against me, my heart shall not fear; though war may rise against me, in this I will be confident. One thing I have desired of the LORD, that will I seek: That I may dwell in the house of the LORD all the days of my life, to behold the beauty of the LORD, and to inquire in His temple. For in the time of trouble He shall hide me in His pavilion; in the secret place of His tabernacle He shall hide me; He shall set me high upon a rock.* Psalm 27:3–5

God did more than Paul could have conceived. He will do a great work in the midst of *your* storm as well.